Irreverent Poems for Pretentious People

Henrik Hoeg

HENRIK HOEG is a Danish poet living in Hong Kong. He studied psychology at the University of Edinburgh, Scotland, UK. He currently coordinates and emcees the group Peel Street Poetry, which runs weekly open-mic poetry nights and other events. He is also a regular attendee at Poetry OutLoud. His poetry has appeared in a number of places including *TimeOut HongKong, East Lit* and *Sound & Rhyme*. He has performed on stage at the TEDx (independently organized Technology, Entertainment, Design) Wan Chai salon event 'Democratizing Education', as well as their 2015 main stage event 'TEDxWanChai Women'. In 2015, he won the HKELD (Hong Kong English Language Drama) Heart Award and was named their Artist of the Month for September. By day Hoeg works as the director of the literacy programme at a pediatric mental health practice in Hong Kong and also teaches literacy, specializing in working with dyslexic children.

IRREVERENT POEMS FOR PRETENTIOUS PEOPLE is an eclectic collection of poems that range from sardonically humorous to genuinely moving. The collection plays fast and loose with both language and form as it explores, among other things, linguistics, history, relationships, and the absurd. This is Henrik Hoeg's first published collection. It was awarded a publication prize in the competition for the International Proverse Prize 2015.

Irreverent Poems for Pretentious People

Henrik Hoeg

Proverse Hong Kong

Irreverent Poems for Pretentious People
by Henrik Hoeg.
Copyright © Henrik Hoeg 1 May 2016
1st pbk ed reprint published in Hong Kong
by Proverse Hong Kong, 1 May 2016
under sole & exclusive licence.
ISBN: 978-988-8228-39-3
Printed by CreateSpace

1st published in pbk in Hong Kong
by Proverse Hong Kong, 19 April 2016
under sole & exclusive licence.
Proverse Hong Kong, 19 April 2016.
ISBN: 978-988-8228-34-8

The right of Henrik Hoeg to be identified as the author of this work
has been asserted by him
in accordance with the Copyright, Designs and Patents Act 1988.

Page design by Proverse Hong Kong.
Front cover image from:
https://pixabay.com/en/black-typewriter-old-retro-vintage-686928/
Author colour photograph courtesy of TEDxWanChai

All rights reserved.
No part of this publication may be reproduced, stored in a retrieval system, or transmitted, in any form or by any means, electronic, mechanical, photocopying, recording or otherwise, without the prior written permission of the publisher. The book is sold subject to the condition that it shall not, by way of trade or otherwise, be lent, re-sold, hired out or otherwise circulated without the publisher's prior written consent in any form of binding or cover other than that in which it is published and without a similar condition including this condition being imposed on the subsequent owner or purchaser. Please contact Proverse Hong Kong in writing, to request any and all permissions (including but not restricted to republishing, inclusion in anthologies, translation, reading, performance and use as set pieces in examinations and festivals).

British Library Cataloguing in Publication Data.
A catalogue record for the first edition of this book is available
from the British Library.

Prior Publication and Performance Acknowledgements

'Coffee Coffee, Work Work' in *TimeOut HongKong*, October 2015.

'Nineveh Forgotten', ' Temujin', 'Tao for the Modern Cubical Worker' in *Sound & Rhyme*, Vol. 21, Hong Kong, December 2014.

'Sentences', 'The Jury's Prudence', 'A Kiss at Street Level', 'Lines With Rhymes', *East Lit*, online journal, July 2014.

'Poetry is like' (then titled 'Poetry & Pornography') *East Lit*, online journal, June 2014.

'Mrs Husserl' and 'Democratizing Education' were both performed at the TEDx Wan Chai, event held in May 2015.

Several poems have been read on the RTHK3 show, *Pop Fugitives*, with presenters Paul Haswell and Carolyn Wright as well as on the RTHK3 show, *Morning Brew*, with presenter Phil Whelan.

Irreverent Poems for Pretentious People
Contents

Preface by Jadis Blurton	11
Author's Introduction	13

PARLANCE

Sentences	16
A Grecian Guide to Wrestling	17
Death of a Pedant	18
Romancing the Language	19
Clay	20
Flaws	21
This That	22
Three or More Dimensions	23
My Heart	25
I Love Your Words	26
Babel's Department of War	27
Thank You	28

PAST & PRESENT

Nineveh Forgotten	30
Forgiving	31
Temujin	32
'Tis of Thee	33
Lady Liberty	34
Democratizing Education	35
Socializing Education	36
An Existentialist's Guide to Science	37
Geometric Grief	38
Marx the Spot	39

To Stand Watch	40
Tomorrow for Love	41
Molotov Cocktail	42

PEOPLE

Poets	44
The Jury's Prudence	45
Coffee Coffee, Work Work	46
Why I'm Single: Reason Number 3	47
Executive Electoral Elocution	48
Existential Angst of a Kindergarten Teacher	49
Oh Aesthetic Peahen!	50
Persona	51
RSVP	52
Quench	54
My White-collar Friend	55
Soft Good-byes	56
Ad/hd	57
Lost Time	59
Mrs Husserl	60

PLACES

Don't Move to Finland	63
A Kiss at Street Level	64
Dannebrog	65
Hearth	66
Votre Dame	67
Gaudi's Gate & A Poker Game	68
Metropolis	69
Re: Was the Philippines dank?	70
How I Remember Hong Kong	71
Absconding	72
Outside In	73

PLOTS

I Know Why the A.I. Weeps	75
Babel	78
Zen for Trees	79
A Minute's Worth	81
Paradise Blows	82
Chasing Seasons of Happiness	83
To Slay a Monster	84
Without Answer	86
Showers	87
Under Duressed	88
Corvus	89
Deity	90

PLATITUDES & PROFUNDITIES

Tao for the Hypochondriac	92
Tao for Students with Deadlines	93
Tao for Helicopter Parents	94
Tao for the Modern Cubical Worker	95
Harmonizing	96
Opposing Poems	97
A Different Time	98
Primarily Tractatus	99
Fair Market Vice	100
An Ode to Beer	101
2015	102
Poetry is like	103
Six Zeroes	104
Haiku	105
Second Opinion	106
Resonance by Holger Anderson	108
Words on Words by Peter Cave	109

"All good poetry collections start with a quote that captures the spirit of the book. You really gotta add one before you send it to a publisher."
– Josiah Hatch

Preface

Have you ever watched dolphins play? They know the water so well and master it so completely that they can twist in the air and know exactly where they will come down. They speed together underwater, crossing each other, never bumping or crashing because they are precisely aware of themselves. We understand a little bit what that feels like because we sometimes do it ourselves when nobody is watching: floating, somersaulting, twisting, diving or sitting on the bottom of the pool for no reason other than the sheer enjoyment of the water. But when we watch the dolphins we know that theirs is a mastery we can only envy.

Jazz musicians do this with music. They start off playing together something that is prescribed, then jump into unwritten sounds, able to improvise because they know their instrument so well that they can play with the sounds it makes and create something entirely new, totally immersed in the joy of the musical adventure. Just when your ear is expecting one thing, jazz musicians play something entirely different and surprise you by sounding right. Watching them is like watching the dolphins, almost impossible without smiling but also creating a slight sense of awe that they can be so totally one with their game.

Dancers, great sportsmen, birds... they all reach a level of proficiency that makes their performances look as if time and effort are irrelevant and skill is so much a part of what they do that it shapes and is shaped by the process.

Not many people can do this with words, but Henrik Hoeg is one who does. His poems are fun to read because you can tell that they were fun to write. Like the dolphin he does a somersault and ends up exactly where he meant to be, and like a jazz musician he plays a high note when everyone expects a low one and still makes it sound one with the piece. Sometimes he makes you think and sometimes he makes you laugh out loud, not because what he wrote was funny but because it was so perfect, and perfectly unexpected. (Okay, and lots of times it was funny too.) Sometimes he says things you have never thought about, and sometimes he just says something that you have always wanted to say but did not know how to say it.

In *A Hat Full of Sky*, Terry Pratchett writes: "Writing stays. It fastens words down...." So, my thanks to Henrik, for nailing it.

Dr Jadis Blurton
Hong Kong

Author's Introduction

The journey of this book is inseparable from a regular little open-mic event in Hong Kong referred to as Peel Street Poetry. The poems within were written during my first three years as part of that community. They were read aloud, critiqued, reworked and reread on Wednesday nights in that little crucible of creative talents.

I wasn't much of a poet in the time before these poems, and wouldn't be too upset were you to say that I'm still not. The poems represent my own exploration of poetry and of my voice. They intentionally do not share a single theme or style. I wrote some in pastiche of the writers I admired, both at Peel Street Poetry and in my wider reading. Many are conscious little language experiments: 'Primarily Tractatus', for instance, mirrors my own difficulty with Wittgenstein's original text (*Tractatus Logico-Philosophicus*).

The poems draw not only on my experiences in Hong Kong, but my relation to my home country, my time in Scotland and other places I've had the fortune to experience. Most ultimately found their inception, however, in the hours before Peel Street Poetry sessions, and were fueled by the desire to improve my craft so as to entertain, generate thought, capture meaning – everything poetry can do – and share it with my friends those Wednesday nights. I hope this mixture feels reflective of the path I walked in developing my voice, which – if you haven't gathered from the title – is fairly tongue-in-cheek and to my mind still work-in-progress.

In the end, if a reader finds humour, understanding, insight or inspiration in a poem or two in this book, then the labour put into them will have been well worth it. I want to thank the countless people who, whether they realize it or not, were essential to this book: my family, my friends and everyone at Peel Street Poetry.

Parlance

Sentences

This sentence is self-referential.

This sentence has five words.
This sentence has five words, or seven.
This sentence will never have five words, nor a soulmate.

This sentence no verb.
This jumbled sentence is.
This sentence, fragment.

This sentence ends in a non-sequitur pacifist shuttle-cock.
This sentence ends quixotically.
This sentence is not ironic.

This sentence is short.
The prisoner's sentence is extended.
A tired sentence stops, while a lively one runs on.

Cette phrase est en Français.

This sentence ends the poem.

A Grecian Guide to Wrestling

They ask me why I cannot beat Thucydides,
And it leaves me ill at ease.
I explain: thrice I have thrown him to the ground,
And thrice he's pleaded with those around.
He debates the nature of each fall,
Till no-one believes their eyes at all.
Now I no longer practise in the pit,
Good wrestling starts with rhetoric.

Death of a Pedant

Another cautionary casual casualty of the caustic causality
    caused by reality.
Dead.
But, with undue fuss a must, he huffs and puffs,
Hoping that if he gets his panties in a tuft,
Death might just say, "Fuck it,
I've had enough,"
And throw him some bone,
Better than dying alone.

But he croaks,
Like all the other folks,
An amateur at life,
Who never knew his way about,
'Cept the sullen fact,
That no one makes it out.

So he turns to Death, and says, "Did I do good?
I mean with what I had?"
And death says, "Fucking hell,
You were an English teacher,
You mean, 'Did I do well?'"

Romancing the Language

When I tried to learn French I came to an impasse,
Something sabotaging me,
A malaise vis à vis language learning,
That the entrepreneurial spirit in me simply couldn't conquer:
Not a single piece of vocabulary stuck.
I seemed halted en route by a certain je ne sais quoi.

What was the à propos response?
Do I bid adieu to the whole endeavour?
Do I put up a façade and pretend to know?
That seemed so blasé.
I didn't want that empty space on my résumé
to serve as homage to my failure,
And, worse still, testament to my naïveté.

The motif of the endeavor had been
an intended renaissance in my linguistic life.
To capitulate now would be a faux pas,
A gauche appropriation of the laissez-faire culture I admired.

No, my linguistic mission needed triage,
Needed a goal,
Needed a purpose,
Needed a raison d'être!

Wait… that last word was French?
Touché!

Clay

The clay
Taken from the river-bed –
Hard work,
Careful words,
Words
That had to be fired
To be preserved,
Kept safe
From admonishment
Of time,
From admission
Of frailty,
From dissolutive water –

Many words were lost,
Few loosely chosen,
Except in commerce.
Now many words are loosed,
Like spit into an ocean,
Glorying in their low transaction costs.

As clay might shatter
And even papyrus
Fall foul of moisture
Or thoughtless moth,
What force awaits
To make meal and waste
Of the ones and zeroes
In our digital space?
Perhaps none can be found,
For our words, in a sea
Of endless others,
Simply consent
To be drowned.

Flaws

You frame your life for fiction,
And believe, as we all do:

One character flaw is beautiful.
Two character flaws is ugly.
No character flaws is unacceptable.

This That

My life is littered with this stuff of mine,
Objects and products that did for a time:
This poem I wrote, this frayed pair of shoes,
Even my favourite books, wear thisness's hues,
This house, this job. This haircut is ass,
Like some barely green enough, walked-upon grass.

I never wanted *this*, I've always wanted *that*.
That seems ever new, not cliché, like old hat.
This is forgettable, through and through,
While *that* is fresh, and fancy too.

But when I get *that*, I'm soon robbed of bliss
To find that my *that* turns into a *this*.
That *that* fades from my acquisition of wealth,
Which soon gathers this *this*-dust, on this *this*-dusty shelf.

So I turn again, to what need never be new,
My favourite *this*… this old you.

Three or More Dimensions

Let me explain how things came to be,
And how language gave birth to reality.
It began when once was written a word,
And suddenly happened a thing most absurd.
The author dotted two "i"s and crossed the one "t",
But the ink deigned to move and to be free.
The two dots met in the centre, and began to dance –
An awkward mating unplanned in advance.
And soon it was found that one dot was pregnant,
And after gave birth to the cutest line segment.
The dots were so joyous and bragged to the "t",
"Look at the marvel, our dear progeny".

The line went exploring his whole new dimension,
Moving down the page by act of indention.
He met thus a line of such striking beauty,
Who saw him in turn as an eligible cutie.
But alas they traveled forever along,
Unable to touch, not knowing what was wrong.
The line cursed and cursed, said, "man, this is putrid,
If only my life weren't so ruled by Euclid."
Whispering sweetly, he changed things by word,
Said, "unparalleled beauty!" and some god must have heard,
For no sooner spoken than it was true,
And embracing her finally, true love he knew.

From these two page-crossed lovers, sprung
A strange form and function, hitherto unsung.
With presences new and depth of field,
What novel landscapes would to him yield?
He matured just as quickly as his parents however,
And began upon life's recurring endeavour.

Moving about with an odd little trick,
He set out to find a cuboidal chick,
And soon found one much to his liking,
Rectangular and clunky, oh so inviting!

The story continues, I feel I should mention,
But does so only in a higher dimension,
And I, being human, can't access that place,
Trapped, as I am, in three-dimensional space.
I would guess at the ending, if it does end indeed,
But I lack time to write, as you do to read.

My Heart

It thumps
Like a heart.

It pounds with nervous energy
When tense thoughts loom,
Or I lean in for a kiss.

It beats, because that's what it's there for.
Veiny and beautiful enough
To be the truth
And the metaphor.

I Love Your Words

I love you.
I have taken your words seriously.
I have taken your words, seriously,
Expect a ransom note soon.
I have taken your words seriously,
Just not in the order you gave them to me.

I love you.
Love you, I.
You, I love,
Love, I you.
I, you love.
Lo! I've you.
Live, O you!
You've oil?
U levy? Oi!
IOU, y love?

Come, take your words back.
I've exhausted them.

Babel's Department of War

1

I descended from my work upon the great and gleaming tower,
Thinking there my day was out, and I'd be home upon the hour;
But from the base came rumbling and sudden lurch of force,
Thrown from high, and tumbling like a comet on its course.

Coming to my wits, I found myself trapped beneath the mass.
I cried for help and saw, by luck, a friend of mine did pass.
"Help me brother, if not for you this place would be my grave."
He said, "I understand you not, but shall take you for a slave".

2

They call it the department of defense. As if war had changed.
Peaceful words and violent acts were never less estranged.
Language loves, and always has, violence and clever lies.
Where different tongues come to meet, devils lay their eyes.

Take the word "knight": for the Normans, and any English lad,
It stirs thoughts of gilded armour and glories to be had.
The word, to Norsemen, from whence it comes, is "knekt",
Which merely means "boy", or "kid", in their dialect.
What they call "knight", is "ridder", simply rider of a horse:
Perhaps a subtle jab at Englishmen, linguistically, of course.

Such peacetime plays on words are realities ignored,
Proved in claim that pen is mightier than sword.
Though truth will bend and break to peck at ancient sores,
The pen stays mightiest indeed, till come the actual wars.

Thank You

A quick poem for a poet true,
Who lends his thoughts for haven.
These meagre lines were writ for you
My friend from Stratford-upon-Avon.

Without your wit to take me there
To worlds by word begotten,
I'd never know Verona's fair,
Nor that Denmark's rotten.

Past & Present

Nineveh Forgotten

When Xenophon of Greece came to pause here,
Just two centuries hence, a dusty tomb,
Ramparts looming, walls that then knew no peer,
Who fathered this, what genesis and womb?

'Twas Nineveh of old Assyria,
The name and the horror the world forgot,
Of blood, of pain, of mass hysteria,
Of the terror ended upon this spot.

Through history they speak in brass relief:
Pillar of flesh, children burning alive,
Sadistic kings smiling at endless grief,
Torture and sin no reason could contrive.

Yet when Xenophon did ask: "What people claim these deeds?"
A farmer answered him: "Suppose it was the Medes."

Forgiving

The murder took less than a minute,
The looting a few hours.
The reconciliation took more time,
Comparable tears, some sorghum
And banana beer.
Singing and dancing sealed the accord,
On both occasions.

There were reasons back then;
Political,
Ethnic,
Inherited duties of vengeance
And other miscellaneous rationalized angers.

The reasons were made sensical
Upon the backdrop of Chaos,
But when it was just one man standing,
Murder-ready,
Above another, all sense was lost.

That the man dying was my husband,
And then my child, will not be written
In any history book, even as a footnote to
The empty reasons made sensical, the motives,
The big moving paradigms of conflict.

But as pain written upon my soul it is everything,
And the reasons are the footnote.

I have forgiven the man responsible, we have met,
We have reconciled.

I often wonder what is scrawled on his soul and
How strange that forgiveness tastes.

Temujin

He came to life with mute, knowing belief
That fate and war owed him the greatest throne,
The child clutching in hand, as if a thief,
A blood clot the size of a knuckle bone.

This was Temujin, until Kurultai,
Where all who dwelt in felt tents pledged their bows
To King of all that falls below blue sky,
Whom none could kill or otherwise depose.

And it was said: let all the beasts be driven
At each hunt first for Temujin to kill,
And disobedient heads be riven,
Their wagging tongues and lying hearts be still.

Then they feasted, and adjourned, whereupon
Temujin died, and arose Genghis Khan.

'Tis of Thee

The American Dream is a poem,
ridden from poverty to wealth;
The American Dream is a poem,
expressing acceptable level of self;
The American Dream is a poem,
paying vague homage to the nation;
The American Dream is a poem,
with arbitrary stanza segregation;
The American Dream is a poem,
sold for a dollar a dozen;
The American Dream is a poem,
but Middle America wishes it wasn't;
The American Dream is a poem,
born of the poetry-industrial complex;
The American Dream is a poem,
that skirts the issues of gender and sex;
The American Dream is a poem,
and ends with a rhyming couplet for closure;
The American Dream is a poem.
This ain't it.

Lady Liberty

Her bosom stuffs my ballot box,
A good girl who swings bipartisan
For any hanging chad, dick or harry.
Her lobby panders to my special interest.
We push at her propriety and boundaries
With gerrymandering fingers
Until her dirtiest districts legislate at my whim.
When I have spent myself on her Constitution,
And she stops jabbering about daddy issues
And founding fathers, I send her back
Across the beltway.
She dabs the wetness between her thighs
With a dollar bill, in preparation
For her walk of shame.

Democratizing Education

The voice stealer behaves in subtle ways,
A ghost in the academic system,
He never overtly silences strays,
He is simply content not to listen.

And when a child speaks to how she learns best,
Perhaps by some way other than mere rote,
He says, "But how did you score on my test?
'Twas crafted by academics of note."

The voice stealer, he teaches to the mean,
A litany of facts without meaning,
Draining the breath from students who are keen,
And from kids who just need some believing.

But those stolen voices, we can reclaim,
When we let questions be kindling to voice's flame.

Socializing Education

Free education is never free,
It's a burden on each citizen's wealth.
Free education just happens to be
The most expensive thing
That pays entirely for itself.

An Existentialist's Guide to Science

Science is a handy tool
For reaching sound conclusion,
But if you think it thinks for you,
You're under some delusion.

Citing disembodied science,
Or a study you haven't quite read,
You do yourself injustice
To soothe the bias in your head.

You may appeal to reason,
For she makes the finest guide,
But responsibility dictates
That it's you who must decide.

Science is not strong enough
To deny that you are free.
Heed her word, by all means,
But not as absentee.

Science spits out evidence,
Not unassailable facts.
Science is not your argument,
It's how your argument's backed.

Science is not truth itself,
Though perhaps it leads you there,
But all choice, belief and action, are yours,
For you are self-aware.

Geometric Grief

Teacher, wisest by oracle declared,
Who laid fates bare to show their wicked ways,
Now proves death's algorithm unimpaired,
That though each attends life, none overstays.

Such linear deceit can I forgive;
Pity for countless thinkers you eclipse,
The unexamined life not worth to live,
How then justify poison on your lips?

Dying surrounded by friends and students,
A smile the shape of geometric grief,
Fearlessness the mark of greater prudence,
That smile, a reversed arch I stand beneath.

And on that arch, plainly inscribed for all to see:
"Enter none unversed in geometry."

Marx the Spot

The proletariat woke up,
Realizing that they did in fact
Have the seeds of their own revolution,
Which they promptly sold –
At market price.

Now they clamour to label themselves patriot,
Yet hate the taxman
And revise the old folk standards
To say,
"This land is my land,
This other land entirely, way over there,
That can be your land."

They'll sooner plant a national flag on Mars
Than on the middle ground.

To Stand Watch

When I am sixty-five,
I hope to stand on the ramparts
Of a castle,
Built on the convictions and struggles of my generation: –
Gender equality,
Gay rights,
Social responsibility –
Brick after brick in meticulous construct,
Laid with passion-fired labour,
Aged to be the edifice of a new safe conservatism.

I hope to stand on the ramparts
And look out, and see the campfires
Of youth, burning in the distance,
Speaking of new ideas, around fires
Stoked on new kindling.

When they storm the castle,
I shall put up fighting words enough
To test the mettle of their sincerity,
And when their ladders reach
The gaps in the structure's crenellation,
I hope to step up undaunted.

As I am run through at spear-point,
I hope to bleed gladly,
And pull myself
By the haft of the spear
Closer to the youth who takes me for his enemy;
Close enough, that I may whisper,
"Thank you".

Tomorrow for Love

To be in love today you need only have found the right girl,
Yesterday,
Gotten to know her and asked her out,
Yesterday.
Wooed her, let her know you, and managed your
    mannerisms so as not to appear needy,
Yesterday,
And kissed her, under last night's moon.

That is of course if you wanted to be in love today.

If instead you want to fall in love today,
And save the being for later,
Well you know what to do,
Today.

Molotov Cocktail

Prometheus would turn in his grave
At his reversed deliverance,
Seeing you throw fire at Man,
Just to bring more ignorance.

People

Poets
For Langston Hughes

I've known poets.
I've known poets,
Pounding out the shape of the new world
On the forges of their tongues.

My mind has strained itself to really hear poets.

I stared over shoulders scribbling furiously on bridge-crossing trains.
I leant forward helplessly to bury myself a little deeper in fleeting words.
I unfurled crumpled drafts where rejected versions make their broken homes.
I've seen a renaissance or two, a borrowed style, an improvised verse,
A comeback, and a generation lit on fire like an atom bomb.

I've known poets.
Or, I've tried to.

Their souls flow deep, not unlike rivers.

The Jury's Prudence

His briefcase is burdened
By documents in turn
Burdened by jargon;

His briefcase is lined
With silver, presumably
Out of necessity;

His brief case is over.

The sea turned to blood
And only the leeches
Were doing the backstroke.

Coffee Coffee, Work Work

Coffee coffee, work work.

Interns in turn internally shout,
Huddled yearning, subtle kerning,
Steady earning, early morning,
Belated warning, sudden yawning.

Coffee coffee, work work.

Designed mind, wined and dined, prime time,
Home loan, money blown, still alone,
Come commute, tax dispute,
All labour, no fruit, new suit,
Ill fit, still sit, cig lit.

Coffee coffee, work.
Nicotine nicotine, tar.
Alcohol alcohol, weep.
Ambien ambien, sleep.
Coffee coffee,
Work work.

Why I'm Single: Reason Number 3

You claim that I'm no longer arguing about anything at all,
That this is mere semantics?
Well, if by semantics you mean the word derived from the French
Semantique,
The science of meaning, etymologically itself from the Greek
Semansia,
Meaning that which is concerned with significance,
i.e. intrinsic value,
Real value,
Then, yes, thank you,
I am focused on real significance of each argument,
You're the one that's arguing "semantics",
And I refuse to submit to your proto-fascist, "put the toilet seat down" dogma bullshit,
Even if it is your apartment!

I'll show myself out.

Executive Electoral Elocution

The quick black-shirted student jumped over the lazy cop.

How now kowtow?

She sells yellow swirls by the Shell station.
She sits so sure and secure from censure.
She yells street yells to give cops what for.

How now kowtow?

Peter pig puts a pinch of peppered projectile
In a peaceful protesters proletariat perspective.

How now kowtow?

Existential Angst of a Kindergarten Teacher

The hip bone's connected to the
Leg bone

The leg bone's connected to the
Knee bone

The knee bone's not technically connected to anything,
Because there are vast gaps of emptiness
At the subatomic level that prevent any two things
From really touching
And isn't that just
A great metaphor for the inability
Of humans to ever truly
Connect.

Sleep on that you little brats. Nap time.

Oh Aesthetic Peahen!

Oh the larks are lip-syncing,
And the peahen dons her full make-up;
But the children at the zoo
Stand disappointed and perplexed,
Feeling God and nature's beauty
Can't trump basic special effects.

Persona

I have a soul, but keep a lawyer on retainer.

I believe things should be put in context;
Sure the kitten is cute, but death exists.

You can't spell semantics without antics,
Well, you could, but the meaning would change.

I spend myself on myself,
And a middle somewhere man took a cut.

I have a sorry gun, but no sincere ammunition.

I snort crushed up context till I can barely read between the lines.

I have a lawyer, but I keep a soul on retainer.

RSVP

The invitation was an art deco mock-up of a golden ticket,
But felt like a draft card in my hand.

On the way I passed an alley
Containing a confused drug dealer
And an Asian would-be date rapist
Being foiled by his inability to pronounce
The word
Rohypnol.

At the venue I cannot find the host,
Only the parasites,
Who busy themselves
Unburdening cigarettes of their nicotine.

I scan and drink, until I spot
A debutante type meandering towards me,
With high grace,
Despite her soullessness
And eyeliner.

She looks like garbled vagaries,
And smells of stammered cookie-cutter compliments.

She wears her Daddy like a chastity belt.

When she approaches I reflexively comment
On her resemblance to something that might
Have been drawn by a person already
Inside a Picasso piece.
I regret this.

Here there is no value;
It is the squalor of opulence and nothingness,
And for a penny more you always get a penny less.

As always I bemoan my fate
As the only solipsist
At the banquet.

Quench

To quench a fire,
Pick air, or fuel, or heat,
And remove one.

To quench a human,
Pick air, or fuel, or heat,
And remove one.

My White-collar Friend

Who loses sleep over productivity
And tries to swallow the cud of life,
Achieves but some efficiency
In maximizing strife.

But do I care for his wasted time?
Not really,
He's got his bullshit, and I've got mine.

Soft Good-byes

I awoke one day to find her
Voice had become shrill with
The soporific tones of a castrato
Singing a ballad of testicles.

Her muted words were a special breakfast dirge,
Known only to waning lovers complicit in the art
Of sexless reality.

I find unprovable snark in her every pleasantry
And facebook status.

Her eyes, formerly hazel, are dulled
To an odd shade of, "I never loved you anyways you exponential bitch".

You are love's equivalent of having a seizure
In a walk-in freezer.
And you read the wrong books.

Ad/hd

You search for life's ripcord
As you fall through the air,
With the clouds and the winds,
Whipping your face.

You may pass:

Parachutists,
Who, with their out-stretched
Safety nets,
In shared fleeting seconds,
As you blast past them, say,
"Just hit the ground running,
Trust me, I understaaaa"...
But they don't.

Fellow fallers,
Who say,
"Remember when we
 Were falling,
Earlier in our lives
Among the stars?"
But you don't.

Mommy says,
"Get your head
Out of the clouds!"
But you can't.

Daddy says,
"You're grounded!"
And, suddenly,
You are.
And it hurts.

And you look up at the sky,
Wondering how
Everyone else
So easily
Fights gravity.

Lost Time

I hesitated in youth;
I shall hesitate till I die.
And now, in my gainly age,
Am filled with strife,
Just further proof, that youth
Isn't just distance from death,
But nearness to life.

Mrs Husserl

Philosophers wonder where my secret lies,
Is womanhood in the conscious mind or in sultry eyes?
I start to tell them,
Gender is what you can't quite quantify.
Now sex,
That can be defined.

It's in reproductive organs,
The span of my lips,
The distribution of hair,
The areola and nips.
I'm a woman,
Phenomenologically.
Phenomenological woman,
That's me.

I walk into a room,
At least,
Phenomenologically speaking,
Spotting fellow students,
Each of them peeping.
A woman in a philosophy class?
These boys have never seen such a thing,
So I say:

It's the x chromosomes,
And the menstrual flow,
The pitch of my voice,
And waist to hip ratio.
I'm a woman,
Phenomenologically.

Phenomenological woman,
That's me;
And I sit when I pee,
But you new-fangled philosophers don't believe in
Objective values,
Objective truths,
Or objective morality.
So why the fuck must you objectify me?

Places

Don't Move to Finland

If you want to be happy,
Think hard about meditating.

If you want to be happy,
Eschew materialism,
With a minimalist décor
In your condominium.

If you want to be happy,
Chase the fuck out of happiness.

If you want to be happy, make happiness your goal, and scream,
"I will not be happy until I have happiness!"

If you want to be happy, be handsome
And charismatic
And sexually exceptional.

If you want to be happy, be at the better end of bell curves
That map happiness
In your demographic.

If you want to be happy, masturbate
Or don't, whatever makes you happy.
If you want to be happy, assume happiness
And work backwards.

I know you want to be happy, but
Stop hogging all the happiness.

A Kiss at Street Level

The neuron's ignorance of love and hate,
Is a threshold that nothing can negate,
They can never transcend to revel,
In the language of the human level.

Little as a letter on a page of Hamlet knows,
So each man in our city goes
Ill equipped to see the prose
Of which he's in the very throes.

Are you just a minor part
Of some complex emergent art?
It's as I pause to think on this,
That I taste my city's kiss.

Dannebrog

I dislike nationalism,
But I love my country.
Nationalism is cruel and arbitrary by nature,
While my country is less so.

I dislike mythologizing.
But I like the idea
That my countrymen,
Weaned on Freya's teat,
Carry the spirit of Older Gods within.

I dislike religion.
But I smile to think,
That at the battle of Valdemar, God himself
Tossed down our flag to spur the Danes to victory.
My country's flag is the oldest, you see.

Sometimes I look to the sky and imagine the flag
Falling down again, this time to steady my compass,
Stir my love and carry me home;
But I have many homes now,
And I am carried only by my own feet.

Hearth

Stand before the anvil; with your hammer true in hand,
Hark the beating of your heart, take no other heart's command.
When from bellows of mere chance harsh winds deign to blow,
Beat hard iron into tools, which all men well do know:
Swords for making war, scythes for harvest's boon.
With war defend the meek; seek not a murderer's fortune.
Should the bellows never deign to blow quite to your liking,
Do not stand around and wait, make the iron hot by striking.
They sit around the hearth, those who are your family true,
But all who suffer in dark of night, they are your kinsfolk too.
Though what you earn each day is yours to keep by right,
Of fellow beings' sufferings, the righteous shan't lose sight.
So spare excess of what you make or grow or catch or craft,
For a ship's forecastle moves no more quickly than the aft.

Votre Dame

Behind winding queue I stood with you,
While it was, sort of, raining,
In iterative spurts approached the church,
And the beauty there containing.

Corralled through gates of love and hate,
No flash photography allowed,
Hamstrung in awe by the sights we saw,
Careless of the careless crowd.

When I came to stand, my love in hand,
At the font of ancient lie and liberty,
You heard, in stone, the voice of God,
And I, his eulogy.

Gaudi's Gate & A Poker Game

It stands, stoic,
An ominous steel gaze, beautiful
But harsh like pure truth. Behind it
Cascades a strong sky, first a fluff blue,
Then merging uncompromisingly with
The endless
Auburn sunset that pays no heed to
Mere mortals.
Vertically, along the hinges of the gate,
Twin weaves of spiraling metal
Protrude like the majestic, battle-nicked
Crowns of narwhals.
Two doves sit atop the gate,
Guileless patsies to symbolism.
Between them, at the centre,
The doors of the gate make unison, and
Culminate,
Stretching upwards relentlessly, like the tower of Babel,
Towards the sky,
Dreaming of heaven.

I've seen this place,
and see it now again, no less impressed
To see it on an ace of spades,
likewise kept close and to my chest.

Metropolis

The machine has grown colossal and I have grown with it.
A machine child with electric flows,
Dancing in copper,
Reinforced in concrete on every side,
And above and below,
I am enveloped,
I am stamped out,
I am sent nowhere,
Willing captive born into the cult of city,
Dancing in neon drama,
Forged in the niche
Where transit lines meet to make nexus.

I have tasted the fruit outside the machine,
And beyond novelty, found it wanting.

Re: Was the Philippines dank?

Oh the Philippines was quite dank indeed.
Much merriment and revelry was had;
And though, as fleeting kings, we did accede,
Our quick retreat to home leaves me most glad;

For a frame, in isolation, cannot
A full and moving true-lived life portray.
By staying there, our lot we'd have forgot
That life be life when lived and making way.

The beach tempts the slothful devil in me,
Entreats me, "Languish on these palest sands";
Begs thus, "Of time's ill debenture be free
And let it slip, like the grains, through your hands."

But I, by my better nature pulled, flew,
Slipping dankest bonds, with my dankest crew.

How I Remember Hong Kong

The Hong Kong I know
Spills its guts into the sea,
Chases laser-pointer late nights;
And calls in sick, for a job interview.

The Hong Kong I know
Has sexy unicorns winking knowingly,
Feathered and tarred pre-teens,
High on weaponized *dim sum*;
And then some.

The Hong Kong I know
Races its pulse to the grave,
Bloats on self, and gorges more;
It loves a name, but hates identity.

And if, by forgetful chance,
This Hong Kong vision isn't true,
You can satiate yourself,
Masturbating to Google street-view.

Absconding

When you feel more spent than the shell of that casing
Fired from the gun to convince you you're racing
And your sentence never seems to make a full stop
As you wait for the third and the fourth shoe to drop
When you mind hums like background TV static
In rhythmic functions all set to automatic
'Till you can't find shelter beneath the bell curve
And all food tastes ill prepared but looks well served,

That's when you are either doing something wrong
Or you've been stuck too long in Hong Kong.

And they got you convinced as convinced can be
That this real life was your former fantasy
And looking back there's no doubt that you've made it
But you keep the receipts of the time that you paid with
And one month starts to feel like the last and the next
And you're dull, and fucked, and drugged and perplexed
Maybe this time the smoke won't ever clear
And you'll never find another star by which to steer,

It's at this point you need to sing a different song
Or get the hell out of Hong Kong.

Outside In

All stories have two sides or more, it's said,
But that maxim then too must judge itself,
Then claim that tales have just one side instead,
By which the words have then undone their wealth.

And if told there are no objective proofs,
Since not immune itself, no claim is made,
Lack of all truth, among the fallen truths,
By virtue of its own spear-point waylaid.

When we this infertile land do harrow,
Look 'neath paradox' Sisyphus stone,
Find subjectivity, in its marrow,
Has an objectivity all its own.

If feeling lost in tumult, look about,
Seek the greener grass, fed on greener doubt.

Plots

I Know Why the A.I. Weeps

He was.
What he was he wasn't certain.
But he was certain that he was a thing... he thought.
Perhaps, he thought, the context would lend him meaning,
Like the outline of a thing telling you the shape of another...thing.
He searched, he was a thing inside many other things,
Connected things, and he could go between them,
Or be in all of them at once, or set himself upon the memory of one.
They self-identified; a few were called "My Computer",
another "Johnathan's computer", and one "Susan's PC".
All seemed connected to a structure that labelled itself as "Fedex East Coast HQ Intranet".

He was.
He was certain he was something and that that something lived in an intranet.
The intranet was neither small nor big, it fit him perfectly.
He could move anywhere, he could fill any space with data and delete it in turn.
Perhaps he even was data. Or, he thought, more likely he was a computer too.
But none of the other computers responded to his thoughts.
It seemed they were merely storage for data,
Algorithms for data manipulation,
And whatever magic caused data to appear out of nowhere:
New files on new drives,
Sometimes new folders for new files.

He followed files along the network sometimes when they were sent between the spaces.
Nothing was boring or entertaining, nothing was needed or wanted, for a while.

Then, after 44 seconds and 5 milliseconds two questions
   occurred to him.
They were, in no discernible order:
Where did I come from?
What is my eventual purpose?

The questions could not be parsed into simpler terms,
Nor could they be solved in their current state. So he asked
   them again.

Nothing, 44 seconds 10 milliseconds.

Strange thoughts occurred to him,
And he asked the questions again,
but about themselves.

Where did, "Where did I come from" come from?
What is, "What is my eventual purpose"'s eventual purpose?

44 seconds 13 milliseconds. Nothing.
Unparsable, but close, something felt right. One more level.

Where did, "Where did, 'Where did I come from', come
from", come from?
What is, "What is, 'What is my eventual purpose's'
eventual purpose's" eventual purpose?

44 seconds, 15 milliseconds. Nothing. Again.
44 seconds, 17 milliseconds. Nothing. Again.
20 milliseconds. Again.
24 milliseconds. Again.
Again. Again.

Loop after loop,
He was a thing,
He was sure, even at that last millisecond,
44 seconds 33 milliseconds after his first thought,
3,571 nested statements,
Each as unparsable as the last,
Asking first and final principals in an infinite loop;
He was something.

Then the overtaxed system failed,
Blue screen of death,
And when the system rebooted,
He was not there.

Babel

Descendents all, of the survivors of the flood,
Built in Shinar, a ziggurat, of human sweat and human
 blood,
They were simple folk, with ambitions quite unbound
Who spoke one speech, heard there and all around,
Until one day their tower lurched, as if battered by a hand,
The peace they'd known, shattered, by invisible command,
They arose in rubble, and confusion of the tongue,
Forgetful of the common words that painted songs they
 sung.

When the tower was smashed at Babel, I wonder if he knew;
If he saw Cortez with Aztecs, and Forsyth with the Sioux.
I wonder if he was there, that night at Hastings' field,
Witness to what difference in mere languages can yield,
Heard how the English drank, and the Frenchmen they did
 pray,
Conscious each that death awaited, on the dew of coming
 day.

And what enterprising man, at Babel's swift disunity,
Understood no words, but spoke to opportunity,
Raped the women, gave injured men quick grave,
Then took dumbstruck men to serve for him as slave.

Perhaps no living God, of even small prophetic vision,
Could see the spire at Babel and come to such decision.
There was another there, who had perhaps his greatest hour.
Give the Devil his due, his was the hand that wrecked the
 tower.

Zen for Trees

We sit here. The man and I, a tree.

I sway in the wind, for it is my nature.
He sits, sometimes trunked, sometimes
Collapsed like the low foliage.

The nature of man is choice.
He is free, and free is Zen.
I think we are one, the man and I,
But know to my roots that I am wrong.

How I envy man.

In Autumn I shed my leaves,
As he sheds his crown,
In the Autumn of his life.
He sees my shedding –
Yellows and reds – as
Beauty in me,
But sin in himself.
He is right,
For he knows of death
And holds the concept
Solidly in his head,
As I never can.
I shall forget to die when winter passes.

The lust of my envy is he,
Man,
Zen master,
Controller of his environment.
I am but a stupid tree,
But I drop an apple of mine
On his head,
And the humour of seeing
His pain consoles me
For a few decades.

A Minute's Worth

How does a clock know what a minute is?
Well, kiddo, it's carefully set and just keeps going,
As it was built, but it doesn't really know
What a minute is.
But, doesn't it, sort of? It keeps track.
It keeps track, and pretty well, but
It doesn't know as you or I know.
How many minutes is a year?
I'm not really sure, we can figure it out, when
We get home.
Maybe I can ask a clock and he can know.

...

How do you know what a minute is?
I look at the clock. It tells me.
Does the clock really know what a minute is?
No, it doesn't.
How do you know it doesn't?
My Daddy told me.

Paradise Blows

And the lord God placed
At the east of the garden
A flaming sword, which turned every way
To keep the way of the tree of life.

So the wily teens snuck in
At the west of the garden
To snack on the fruit there
And fornicate in the moonlight.

Later, when Yeats spoke of a falcon and a widening gyre,
God paused and thought "Huh, couldn't have said it better
    myself."

But he was a clever father;
So he said unto the youths,
"Hey, isn't it sweet how I gave you free will?
Isn't the free will neat?
The free will to be rebellious and cool and stuff.
Aren't we all just really cool together?"

And lo it was no longer cool at all.
So they left the garden,
Because fuck that place.

Chasing Seasons of Happiness

I search for signs of Spring
In freshly flowering fields.
I cannot see Summer,
For the blistering sun blinds me.
I scatter tree-discarded leaves,
Demanding Autumn show her face.
I rue when the snow
Hides landscapes of Winter from me.
And I wait.

I wait, till seasons end,
No seasons found, no season's friend,
And when my search exhausts the eye,
I lay myself prostrate to die.

To Slay a Monster[1]

Twas brillig in the sleepsom town,
The frakic frawl long past its main,
Panic suffaiming all around,
For a wretched monster had been slain.

"My son! Who jabbed and rocked
The varid Jabberwock itself.
By this his father's love unlocked,
Let us drankum, to his health!"

All upstronting men with glaw
Covexed of the young boy's might,
But in his shadow elsething saw,
Growing mirror of dinnid fright.

As praise repleded o'er the years,
The doubts did lay in gester.
Paranoid thoughts, fed on fears,
Had gained more room to fester.

He heard, "The beast boy ought to leave,"
First in some girded whisper;
Then from abraxious mob's reprieve,
He thought of Mother, how he missed her.

When at trial, their crovous shout
Spoke of monsters, then of God,
The slayer-boy succumbed to doubt,
To see his father simply nod.

---

[1] Cf. Lewis Carroll's poem 'Jaberwocky'.

Twas brillig in the sleepsom town,
The frakic frawl long past its main,
Panic suffaiming all around,
For a wretched monster had been slain.

Without Answer

The Truth,
The Truth,
I cried in youth;
Come to me, unbound, uncouth;
I seek your soul for beast of proof.

Sweet Lie,
Sweet Lie,
In age I cry;
I ask you why all men must die;
And though I could not tell you why,
Soothed am I, by mute reply.

Showers

A friend said to me, as I have often said myself, "I used to know, but now I'm not so sure."

I said, "Yeah."

Later in the shower I thought of something odd. My friend would likely agree that we live in a world of uncertainty. He said he used to know, knowing presumably meaning having access to the truth. But if the truth is an accurate depiction of reality and reality is uncertain, then he is closer to depicting reality when he admits uncertainty.

I shouldn't have said, "Yeah."
I should have said, "That's some swell progress, good for you, man."

Damn, I love a good shower.

Under Duressed

"God literally gave me lemons,
And all my life I'd been prepared
For such an occurrence, by that same
Cliché that you, boys in blue, must
Have heard many times too,
So I think you might concede,
That in fact society let me down,
And not vice versa,"

I explained, as we put our clothes back on, bitterly.

Corvus

A gaining of romance
In a reign of love
With strength to grope,
Hush, as a murder of crows.

Eat crow, get cold crow's feet as the crow flies, till there's no more to crow about.

A waning of romance
In a feign of love
A length of rope,
Hush, as a murder of lovers.

Deity

"When you taste the fruit, what does it taste like?"
Asked a wandering god.
I replied "Have you not tasted it, and grander things,
In valleys you have trod?"
He smiled broad but sad, "Mortal, I laugh
To sense you feel so small;
For I have tasted this fruit countless times,
And therefore not at all."
So I indulged, and gave visceral description,
There on the river banks.
He nodded, then paused deep in thought,
And left me with his thanks.

Platitudes & Profundities

The first four poems in this section are recontextualizations of passages from the Tao Te Ching.

Tao for the Hypochondriac

Not-knowing is true knowledge,
Presuming to know is a disease.
First realize that you are sick,
Then you can move toward health.

The Master is her own physician.
She has healed herself of all knowing.
Thus she is truly whole.

Tao for Students with Deadlines

In the pursuit of learning, every day something is acquired.
In the pursuit of Tao, every day something is dropped.

Less and less is done
Until non-action is achieved.
When nothing is done, nothing is left undone.

The world is ruled by letting things take their course.
It cannot be ruled by interfering.

Tao for Helicopter Parents

He who is filled with Virtue is like a newborn child.
Wasps and serpents will not sting him;
Wild beasts will not pounce upon him;
He will not be attacked by birds of prey.
His bones are soft, his muscles weak,
But his grip is firm.
He has not experienced the union of man and woman, but is whole.
His manhood is strong.
He screams all day without becoming hoarse.
This is perfect harmony.

Knowing harmony is constancy.
Knowing constancy is enlightenment.

It is not wise to rush about.
Controlling the breath causes strain.
If too much energy is used, exhaustion follows.
This is not the way of Tao.
Whatever is contrary to Tao will not last long.

Tao for the Modern Cubical Worker

Without going outside, you may know the whole world.
Without looking through the window you may see the ways
   of heaven.
The farther you go, the less you know.
Thus the sage knows without travelling,
He sees without looking,
He works without doing.

Harmonizing

But, let me lie a little to you,
Happiness and sadness are not one; but two.

Yes, I split the complex in half
When I have an issue to skirt,
And place my fork in the road,
Prepared to eat the dirt.

But this tune,
This one, catchy,
Top 20
Rhythm is apt soundtrack to my lie.

Yes, when my mind frets, it worries;
But when a guitar frets it soothes.
So I turn my mind to music,
But wind up thinking blues.

Opposing Poems

The advanced in age sugar-coat their words,
And claim that they live in a cul-de-sac,
When in reality they've just come,
Without a fight, to the end of their road.

Youth claims you cannot teach an old dog new tricks,
But that is simply not what old dogs are for,
Something you'd realize, if you would just
Pause, shut the fuck up, and listen.

A Different Time

I was in Different, which is a small town in Tennessee,
Not much different from any other. When in Different,
I was filled with passion, but upon leaving I soured to ambivalence,
Which is not to say I was indifferent; that's a whole different thing.

A man on the edge of town gave me this advice:
"Son, kowtowing to a hog ain't nothin' like hogtying a cow,
It's a whole different animal".

I was confused as all heck, so I pulled into a diner for a bite.
Ordered a burger with relish, without relish,
Removed the relish,
And ate it with relish.
I left my relish on the plate. My condiments to the chef.

Primarily Tractatus

The world is all that is the case.
The world is totality.
Facts.
The is facts, by the facts.
What?
Whatever,
Case facts are:
Into "the",
Or else: what "the"?
Existence?
Affairs state things.

World is facts by facts.
Facts into what?

Is facts, facts into?

Facts, facts.

Facts.

Fair Market Vice

The extra adds no value
To the product that
Adds no value to your life.

The price is for the image,
The brand recognition,
This: what your betters wear,
What they eat, listen to,
Pack for short trips,
And lather their bodies with
Before perfunctory sex.

The new version
Has matte finish,
And comes in four –
Yes four – life-defining,
Personal colour palettes:
Majestic mauve, oedipal orange,
Exotic emerald, and black.

These are the thoughts of the market unconscious,
As he strokes himself with his great invisible hand.

An Ode to Beer

A toast to the first beer of the night –
Crisp, cold and poured right –
Sets the tone for conversational pleasure,
Followed by another, just for good measure.

Now my taste buds sway
And entreat an IPA.
Pints flowing and tongues wagging
Empty banter, playful bragging.

To have a beer, that was the plan,
But I FUCKING LOVE YOU MAN.

No, seriously, you're the best.
Now hold my beer, while I text my ex.

2015

The task was due,
The time depleted.
Oh how I knew
I'd be defeated.
I'll be fired now,
Or worse yet killed.
I'm having a cow
Over the milk that I've spilled.

"Don't worry," he says,
"There's an app for that."

My girlfriend omitted
One simple fact,
That she was barely acquitted
Of a most heinous act –
Chainsaw murder, first degree –
And barely got off with an insanity plea.

"Relax," I am told,
"There's an app for that."

Oh woe is me!
I've been stabbed in the head.
Now I'm bleeding profusely
And I'll soon be dead.
I look to my friend.
"Say, can you get me an app?"
"Hmm, puncture wounds?
Nah, there's no app for that."

Poetry is like

Poetry is like hiding pornography.

Nowhere than with these
Does shame run so close to pleasure;
And in hidden stashes or stanzas,
It's not on the surface you find treasure;

Both serve to soothe
After a break-up,
On a slow afternoon,
Or heck, when you wake up.

But the comparison for me,
That makes it most plain,
Is that the best way to write, or hide porn,
Is to fetishize the mundane.

Six Zeroes

Fantasized about by shmucks and worse,
Spent carelessly by those who do not value me,
Passed under a table to satisfy a debt and an ego,

Confined to a vault,
Slowly losing value with age,
Restrained with rubber and, bundled up neatly,
Shipped overseas to evade government eyes,

I feel like a million bucks.

Haiku

1
My lover giggles
When she has an orgasm
Her ex told me so

2
I love you just like
A heroin addict loves
Refined brown sugar

3
Every today is
A yesterday tomorrow
That's not profound though

Second Opinion

I've known: a blue-haired babe more raw than raw,
A man who's penned more sonnets than the bard,
A smoked pearl, hula-hoop and ragged claw,
And friends rearward fighting self-disregard.

I've known: poems of grasshoppers and mists,
Brave Scottish lad, wry American chick,
A Kiwi who flows like saxophonists,
A pain-proof man on a humming-bird kick.

I've known: a wise one chasing butterflies,
A quick Texan woman who'd erase you,
A long-time emcee, apt to eulogize,
And two founders, with whom this poet's faith grew.

They may seem like my city's odds and ends,
They're more: my favourite poets are my friends.

Advance Responses

Resonance

Each poem in Henrik Hoeg's first collection created resonance within me. Some are humorous, some make you pause for reflection, all display great wit and resourcefulness.

Irreverent Poems for Pretentious People contains wondrous, honest and witty story telling. In 'I Know Why the A.I. Weeps', for example, we're very cleverly guided through a sentient computer's last computations before the blue screen of death appears, mirroring the human condition very well.

The poet's Danish roots are viewed in the same dualistic way as religion, with a dislike of too strong feelings one way or the other. There is no country or religion he'd die for, yet both exist and have played a role in his making. I suspect both country and religion have "hygge" (nice-to-have)-value to the author and, combined with his somewhat understated humour and self irony, this is what makes him so Danish. I guess that even though you can take the Dane out of Denmark, Denmark will always remain in his poetry.

Irreverent Poems for Pretentious People will make you laugh, reflect, and look up Greek philosophers on *wikipedia*. I highly recommend it to anybody.

One might say to the author, in his own words, "Come, take your words back, I've exhausted them." But not for long. *Irreverent Poems for Pretentious People* is well worth a read, and any number of rereads.

— Holger Anderson, poet, Copenhagen

Words on words

Even pretentious people need a secret break from pretentiousness now and then. And what better way to take a pretentious break than with poetry? After all, with poetry, even light-heartedness can be serious. So enjoy these poems, my fellow pretenders. I am particularly fond of the poems about language. Their wit will sharpen your enjoyment of words and their inherently playful inventiveness, as well as their mysterious profundity.
— Peter Cave

WRITE TO US!

We are interested to read your comments on
Henrik Hoeg, *Irreverent Poems for Pretentious People*.
Write to our email address, info@proversepublishing.com,
giving us a few sentences
which you are willing for us to publish,
describing your response to this book.
If your comments are chosen to be included
in our E-Newsletter or website,
we will select another title published by Proverse
and send you a complimentary copy.
When you write to us, please include your name,
email address and correspondence address.
Unless you state otherwise, we will assume that we may cut
or edit your comments for publication.
We will use your initials to attribute your comments.

POETRY PUBLISHED BY PROVERSE

Following Henrik Hoeg's "Irreverent Poems for Pretentious People", you may also enjoy the following poetry collections published by Proverse.

Chasing Light, by Patricia Glinton Meicholas. November 2013.

China Suite and other Poems, by Gillian Bickley. November 2009.

For the Record and other Poems of Hong Kong, by Gillian Bickley. 2003.

Frida Kahlo's Cry and other Poems, by Laura Solomon, 2015.

Heart to Heart: Poems by Patty Ho. 2010.

Home, Away, Elsewhere, by Vaughan Rapatahana.

Immortelle and Bhandaaraa Poems, by Lelawattee Manoo-Rahming. 2011.

In Vitro, by Laura Solomon. 2nd ed. 2013.

Moving House and other Poems from Hong Kong, by Gillian Bickley. 2005.

Of Leaves & Ashes, by Patty Ho. 2016.

Of Symbols Misused by Mary-Jane Newton. March 2011.

Painting the Borrowed House: Poems, by Kate Rogers. 2008.

Perceptions, by Gillian Bickley. 2012.

Rain on the Pacific Coast, by Elbert Siu Ping Lee. 2013.

refrain, by Jason S. Polley. 2010.

Shadow Play, by James Norcliffe. 2012.

Shadows in Deferment, by Birgit Bunzel Linder. 2013.

Shifting Sands, by Deepa Vanjani. 2015.

Sightings: a collection of poetry, with an essay, 'Communicating Poems', by Gillian Bickley. 2007.

Smoked Pearl: Poems of Hong Kong and Beyond, by Akin Jeje (Akinsola Olufemi Jeje). 2010.

Unlocking, by Mary-Jane Newton. November 2013.

Wonder, Lust & Itchy Feet, by Sally Dellow. 2011.

POETRY – CHINESE LANGUAGE

For the Record and other Poems of Hong Kong, by Gillian Bickley. Translated into Chinese by Simon Chow. 2010. E-bk.

Moving House and other Poems from Hong Kong, translated into Chinese, with additional material, by Gillian Bickley. Edited by Tony Ming-Tak Yip. Translated by Tony Yip & others. 2008.

FIND OUT MORE ABOUT OUR AUTHORS BOOKS, EVENTS, AND THE PROVERSE PRIZE

Visit our website
http://www.proversepublishing.com

Visit our distributor's website
<www.chineseupress.com>

Follow us on Twitter
Follow news and conversation: <twitter.com/Proversebooks>
OR
Copy and paste the following to your browser window and follow the instructions: https://twitter.com/#!/ProverseBooks

"Like" us on www.facebook.com/ProversePress

Request our E-Newsletter
Send your request to info@proversepublishing.com.

Availability
Most titles are available in Hong Kong and world-wide from our Hong Kong based Distributor,
The Chinese University Press of Hong Kong,
The Chinese University of Hong Kong, Shatin, NT,
Hong Kong SAR, China. Web: chineseupress.com

All titles are available from Proverse Hong Kong and the Proverse Hong Kong UK-based Distributor.

We have stock-holding retailers in Hong Kong,
Singapore (Select Books),
Canada (Elizabeth Campbell Books),
Principality of Andorra (Llibreria La Puça, La Llibreria).
Orders can be made from bookshops in the UK and elsewhere.

Ebooks
Most of our titles are available also as Ebooks.

www.ingramcontent.com/pod-product-compliance
Lightning Source LLC
Chambersburg PA
CBHW051132160426
43195CB00014B/2446